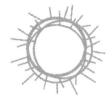

Forgiven

RESURRECTION MEDITATIONS
FROM THE BOOK OF HEBREWS

TIM CHESTER

10 Publishing
a division of 10ofthose.com

British Library Cataloguing in Publication Data
A record for this book is available from the British Library

ISBN: 978-1-914966-15-6

Designed and typeset by Pete Barnsley (CreativeHoot.com)

Printed in Demnark by Nørhaven

10Publishing, a division of 10ofthose.com
Unit C, Tomlinson Road, Leyland, PR25 2DY, England

Email: info@10ofthose.com
Website: www.10ofthose.com

1 3 5 7 10 8 6 4 2

Introduction

We live in uncertain times. We've discovered how an unknown illness can turn our world upside down out of the blue. Our society is changing rapidly and many of us feel left behind. Older people can't keep up with dramatic cultural shifts while young people have little prospect of economic security.

Into this mix come our own personal challenges – our fear, guilt, shame and insecurity. Every sin we commit makes us wonder if we have a future with God. Every wrong we receive makes us wonder if he cares.

How can we face the future with confidence? The writer of Hebrews reassures our fearful hearts by pointing us to the Lord Jesus. One of his favourite words is *'confidence'*. He invites us to find in Christ the confidence of a clear conscience (9:14; 10:22; 13:18) and the confidence to approach God (4:16; 7:19; 10:19, 22; 13:6).

The opening chapters of the letter explore the *identity* of Jesus. They show how Jesus is the final word from God (1:1–2), the heir of all things (1:2), the creator of the universe (1:2), the radiance of God's glory and the exact representation of his being (1:3), the king who is superior to angels (1:5–13), the true humanity (2:5–9), the pioneer of salvation (2:10), and our faithful high priest (2:17–18; 4:14–5:10). Above all, Jesus is the eternal Son of God (1:2). That was the focus of the precursor to this book, *Fixated: Advent Meditations from the Book of Hebrews* (10Publishing).

The second half of Hebrews explores the *work* of Jesus. The letter describes what Jesus has accomplished along with what he continues to be doing now that he has ascended into heaven. The writer invites us to find deep assurance in the finality of Christ's work on earth. His sacrifice was 'once for all' (7:27; 9:12, 26; 10:11). So there is nothing left to be done and nothing that can become undone. The writer also invites us to find deep assurance in the on-going work of Christ. Christ remains as committed to us as ever. His forever intercession as our high priest secures our salvation forever.

So Hebrews 6–13 will be the focus of this book. It offers a great way of approaching Easter by inviting us to look deeper at the cross and find a new confidence to face the future.

Chapter 1

Jesus is the Firm Anchor
(Hebrews 6)

Imagine a university student who can't read or a teenager living on baby food. Or imagine a soccer player who keeps wildly kicking at the ball rather than picking out a good pass. This is how the writer describes his readers:

- They are like pupils who have never got beyond the basics (5:12).

- They are like children who still live on milk (5:12–13).

- They are like athletes who never bother to practise (5:14).

It's not that they're stupid. The problem is 'you no longer try to understand' (5:11). The same word is used again in 6:12 where it's translated 'lazy'. They're not learning because they're distracted by other things. Jesus has slipped down their list of priorities.

It's time to move forwards, says Hebrews: 'Therefore let us move beyond the elementary teachings about Christ and be taken forward to maturity' (6:1). The writer describes the ABCs of Christianity that his readers ought to have under their belt. 'Cleansing rites' (literally 'baptisms') and 'the laying on of hands' are probably references to baptism and church membership. And 'cleansing rites' are plural because for his Jewish readers this 'instruction' would include how baptism supersedes Old Testament cleansing rites. So the elementary teachings are:

- Repentance and faith – the *internal* responses we make to Christ.

- Baptism and church membership – the *outward* responses we make to Christ.

- Resurrection and judgment – what's at stake when we respond to Christ.

Now the writer exhorts us to go beyond 'Christianity 101' and take a class in *'maturity'* or more literally *'perfection'* (6:1). We're to move towards perfection. Does it mean we've got to be perfect? No, that's an impossible standard. This letter is littered with references to perfection. Hebrews talks about Jesus as a 'perfect' priest (7:28) who enters a 'perfect' sanctuary (9:11) through a sacrifice that makes 'perfect' (10:1). So this is not a call to live a perfect life. It's a call to press deeper into Christ. Moving forward to perfection means 'fixing our eyes on Jesus, the pioneer and *perfecter* of faith' (12:2).

Reflection

Is it time for you to move forwards in some way?

Going backwards   Hebrews 6:4–12

The interpretation of verses 4–6 is much disputed. Some people think they show Christians can forfeit their salvation. Because elsewhere the Bible teaches that God will keep his people to the end (Phil. 1:6; Jude 24), other people argue that warnings like this are one of the ways God keeps us. But I think the writer is describing people who have experienced God in some way without ever truly turning to Christ in faith and repentance. Perhaps they've understood the message ('been enlightened') or taken communion ('tasted the heavenly gift') or been miraculously healed ('shared in the Holy Spirit') or been moved by a sermon ('tasted the goodness of the word of God'). But they've never personally entrusted themselves to Christ.

Verses 7–8 echo the parable of the sower (Mk. 4:1–20). Sometimes the seed of God's word falls on rocky ground or among thorns. Initially it springs up. But it withers when troubles come or is overwhelmed by the attractions of this world because it's never really taken root in a person's heart.

A Satnav will often give you two or three possible routes to your destination: a route without toll roads, perhaps, or one with fewer turns. But there is no alternative route that avoids the need for faith and repentance. If you reject faith in Christ then there is no option B. There is no other way to be saved.

It's a sombre warning to entrust yourself to Christ in faith and submit your life to him in repentance. It's no good hanging around the fringes of church life. It's no good relying on the faith of your parents or spouse. You need to make your own decision to follow Christ. And coming to the front at a meeting many years ago counts for nothing if you're not living a life of faith and repentance today.

But if you have entrusted yourself to Christ then there is no need to worry. Your salvation does not hang in the balance. The writer says to his readers: 'we are convinced of better things in your case – things that have to do with salvation' (v. 9). He's going to give them even more reasons to reassure them in verses 13–20.

Reflection

Through 'faith and patience' we will 'inherit what has been promised' (v. 12).

God doesn't want us to live in doubt. 'God wanted to make the unchanging nature of his purpose very clear,' says verse 17. He wants us to have assurance. He wants us to be confident about the future. So God confirmed his promise with an oath.

'I'm telling the truth,' we say. 'I swear on my mother's grave.' As children we used to say, 'Cross my heart, hope to die, stick a needle in my eye.' At a more serious level, a witness in court says, 'I swear by Almighty God that the evidence I shall give shall be the truth, the whole truth and nothing but the truth.' We swear an oath to confirm that our words are true.

God didn't need to confirm his promises with an oath because 'it is impossible for God to lie' (v. 18). It ought to be enough for God to make a promise. That's reason enough to trust him. We make oaths because human beings are notoriously untrustworthy. So all too often our word is not enough. But God is always faithful. He always delivers. He cannot lie.

But so that we can be *doubly sure*, God also swore an oath. We have his promise and we have his oath – 'two unchangeable things' (v. 18). 'People swear by someone greater than themselves,' says verse 16. But there is nothing greater than God. So God 'swore by himself' (Gen. 22:16–17). God put his own reputation on the line.

God didn't have to do this. His word should have been enough. But 'God wanted to make the unchanging nature of his purpose very clear' (v. 17). 'God did this so that … we who have fled to take hold of the hope set before us may be greatly encouraged' (v. 18). There are two impossible things in Hebrews 6:

- In verse 4, *'It is impossible'* for those who reject God to be saved.

- In verse 18, *'it is impossible'* for God to reject those whom he has promised to save.

Reflection

If you're living in unrepentant sin then hear the warning in this passage, be afraid and let that fear drive you to Christ. But if you're trusting in Christ then *don't* be afraid. 'Be greatly encouraged,' says verse 18, for it is impossible for God to let you go.

Picture a boat which is kept safe because it's anchored to the ocean bed. The waves are tipping it up and down, and the wind is blowing it towards the rocks. Maybe that's how you feel. The waves of life are tipping you up and down. You feel at their mercy. You're feeling overwhelmed. You fear going under. You feel adrift in the storm.

The good news is that, like our boat, we have an anchor – 'an anchor for the soul' (v. 19). It's the hope we have through the *promises of God*. God has promised to guide us home. Our future is secure. In the midst of the storm we can look ahead to our destination with confidence. One day you may be up and the next day you may come crashing down. But nothing can change your destiny. Your hope is 'firm and secure' (v. 19).

Our hope is secure because of the promise and oath of God. But it's also secure because of *'our forerunner, Jesus'* (v. 20). Jesus has already arrived. He has gone 'behind the curtain' (v. 19). It's an image taken from the tabernacle where the curtain divided the people from the holy presence of God. At his ascension Jesus, as it were, passed through that curtain into God's presence on our behalf. He's now there in heaven as our high priest, representing us before God.

It's as if Jesus has tied himself to you with an unbreakable rope. Then he has gone ahead through the storms of death and planted one end of the rope in heaven. He's anchored it firmly there with his own person. So that now there's no possibility of you ever being swept away. Right now you are tethered to heaven.

When the storms of life threaten to overwhelm you, what should you do? Fix your eyes on Jesus. When your sin and guilt undermine your assurance of salvation, what should you do? Fix your eyes on Jesus. He is the anchor of your soul.

Reflection

When everything around you is turning and churning, Jesus is the *fixed point*. So make him your *focal point*.

Chapter 2

Jesus is the Forever Priest (Hebrews 7)

The American writer Mark Twain is supposed to have sent a telegram to a dozen people saying, 'Flee at once – all is discovered.' They all left town. Imagine you received that message: 'All is discovered.' What's just come into your head? Your eating disorder? Your porn habit? A criminal conviction? Your credit card debt? Some secret shame or sin?

Now think about how that secret affects your relationship with God. Perhaps there are times when you've hesitated to pray. Or times when you feel a fraud. Or times when you doubt your salvation. Perhaps you fear God might give up on you.

What God wants you to know today is this: *Jesus saves you completely and always intercedes for you.* This is the message of Hebrews 7.

The writer starts with an apparent problem. He's already called Jesus our 'great high priest' (4:14). To be the king of Israel you had to be from the tribe of Judah – which Jesus was (7:14). But to be a high priest in Israel you had to be from Levi – which Jesus wasn't. So Jesus can't be both (7:13). Or can he?

Jesus is a different kind of priest from a different kind of priesthood – one from the order of Melchizedek. So who on earth is Melchizedek? You can read about him in Genesis 14:18–20, but Hebrews 7:1–2 tell us most of what there is to know. Abraham had won a battle and on his way home he met Melchizedek. Melchizedek blessed Abraham and Abraham gave him a tenth of the plunder.

Hebrews gives three reasons why Melchizedek resembles the Son of God (v. 3).

- Melchizedek is a king as well as a priest – as his name indicates (v. 2).

- Melchizedek remains a priest forever – at least in the sense that his story has no conclusion (v. 3).

- Melchizedek is greater than the Levitical priests – since they are descendants of Abraham and Abraham paid tribute to Melchizedek (v. 6–7).

Reflection

Jesus is our Priest-King. As 'king of Salem' he brings us peace by rescuing us from sin and death. As our priest he brings us peace by reconciling us to God.

Linking Jesus to Melchizedek as the writer does in verses 1–10 doesn't just solve the problem of how Jesus can be a priest when he's not from the tribe of Levi. It solves a bigger problem – the failure of the Levitical priesthood. 'If perfection could have been attained through the Levitical priesthood,' says verse 11, '– and indeed the law given to the people established that priesthood – why was there still need for another priest to come, one in the order of Melchizedek, not in the order of Aaron?'

The Levitical priesthood was a failure. The problem was not so much that individual priests let the side down. Some did, but many served faithfully. The real problem was that they were part of a *system* that couldn't solve the problem of sin. 'For when the priesthood is changed,' says verse 12, 'the law must be changed also.' In other words, we need a new priesthood because we need a new system.

And that's what we get in Jesus. Jesus is not part of the old system – he's not part of the Levitical priesthood (v. 13–16). Jesus is a new kind of priest from a new kind of priesthood (v. 17). And with a new priesthood we get a new system. This is how the writer puts it in verses 18–19: 'The former regulation is set aside because it was weak and useless (for the law made nothing perfect), and a better hope is introduced, by which we draw near to God.'

The old system of priests and sacrifices (set out in the book of Leviticus) was 'useless'. It's strong language – especially when you think of how many animals died to maintain it over the centuries. And to be fair the old system did its real job – pointing to Jesus – really well.

But what it couldn't do was make anyone perfect. It couldn't deal with sin. It couldn't save God's people. When it came to enabling people to draw near to God 'it was weak and useless' (v. 18).

But now 'a better hope is introduced, by which we draw near to God' (v. 19). And that hope is Jesus.

Reflection

Think of all the animal sacrifices required in the past so people could draw near to God. Today you can pray at any time and in any place without fuss if you *draw near to God* in the name of Jesus.

Jesus is a new and better kind of priest from the order of Melchizedek, and so he offers a better way of drawing near to God.

But at this point you might be thinking, 'Surely you can't just change the rules like this.' Hebrews is one step ahead of you. Jesus is made a priest through a direct edict or oath from God. It's an idea the writer of Hebrews gets from Psalm 110:4.

The story of Melchizedek is told in just three verses in Genesis 14. But it's not the only time we meet him in the Old Testament. He turns up again in Psalm 110:4:

> *The LORD has sworn*
> *and will not change his mind:*
> *'You are a priest for ever,*
> *in the order of Melchizedek.'*

God is speaking to his coming king and declares that he will be a Priest-King like Melchizedek. The writer of Hebrews has already quoted the second half of this verse to show that Jesus is this promised Priest-King (v. 17). In verse 21, he quotes the first half to show that Jesus is our Priest-King by divine decree.

Here's the point: 'Because of this oath, Jesus has become the guarantor of a better covenant' (v. 22).

The new covenant or system for drawing near to God is guaranteed by Jesus and that guarantee is underwritten by God. God himself appoints Jesus as our priest and confirms his credentials (v. 22; 5:5-6, 10). God has sworn on oath that everyone who comes to him in the name of Jesus will receive a warm welcome. And God 'will not change his mind' (v. 21). No wonder verse 19 calls this 'a better hope'.

Reflection

God has sworn on oath that if *you* come to him in the name of Jesus you will receive a warm welcome.

We've already been told that the old system could not make us 'perfect' because it was 'weak and useless' (v. 18–19). But what was the problem? And why does Jesus provide a 'better hope' (v. 19)?

One problem with the Levitical priests is that they never lasted! The very fact that we're talking about 'priests' plural proves the point. They kept having to be replaced. 'Now there have been many of those priests,' says verse 23, 'since death prevented them from continuing in office'. One after another they died! So none of them could offer a permanent solution to the problem of sin. They were always just patching up the wound, but never truly healing it. They were signs pointing to a permanent solution, but none of them could ever be the real thing. 'But,' says verse 24, 'because Jesus lives for ever, he has a permanent priesthood.'

It's an idea that's been rumbling away in the background throughout the chapter:

- 'Without beginning of days or end of life, resembling the Son of God, [Melchizedek] remains a priest for ever' (v. 3).

- Jesus 'has become a priest not on the basis of a regulation as to his ancestry but on the basis of the power of an indestructible life' (v. 16).

Jesus provides a permanent solution for sin because he is a permanent priest, and he is permanent because he is 'indestructible' (v. 16).

Suppose you have a fence that keeps falling down in the wind. So you embed new posts in concrete, but the wood rots. So you drive in metal stakes, but the metal rusts. So finally you get titanium posts. They're indestructible and so at last you can be confident your fence is permanent. Jesus is 'indestructible' and so his solution for sin is permanent.

Perhaps you've bought a gadget that came with a lifetime guarantee. The salvation of Jesus comes with a lifetime guarantee – and verse 24 says 'Jesus lives for ever'.

Reflection

Your salvation will last as long as Jesus lasts, and Jesus is indestructible!

A priest for every sin   Hebrews 7:25

Bottles of detergent often claim to kill 99 per cent of all household germs. At this point I always want to say, 'Tell me about the one per cent? How dangerous are the one per cent of germs that it can't kill?'

In terms of physical health that one per cent might not matter very much. But when it comes to spiritual protection nothing less than 100 per cent will do. Covering 99 per cent of all our sins is not enough – not if we're to be safe forever. Only perfection will do.

Verse 25 says: 'Therefore he is able to save completely those who come to God through him, because he always lives to intercede for them.' The word translated 'completely' is literally 'all-perfect'. Jesus is the perfect solution for every sin. Jesus removes 100 per cent of all known sins and all unknown sins. He removes every stain and cleanses all our guilt.

Instead of the bottle of detergent in our shopping basket, let's look at the stick of deodorant. Perhaps your deodorant claims to provide 24-hour protection. It will protect you from the shame of body odour for a whole day.

The word 'always' (*pantote*) in verse 25 has the same prefix as the word 'completely' (*panteles*). In other words, the solution Jesus offers is *all*-encompassing and for *all*-time. Jesus always saves because he always intercedes.

So Jesus offers 24-hour protection, seven days a week, *for the rest of time*. He makes you clean in *every* moment and for *all* time. Not just your good moments. Not just when you're in church. Not just when you're praying. Not just on your good days. Every moment. Every scenario. Every failure. Every future you might face. Jesus covers every sin forever.

Reflection

Whenever Satan points to your sins as a reason for your condemnation, Jesus points to his wounded hands and side as a better and stronger reason for your forgiveness.

A priest for every sin   Hebrews 7:26-28

The first ever sacrifices for God's people offered by the Levitical priesthood are described in Leviticus 9. It was a great moment. At the end, when the sacrifices had been made, Aaron lifted up his hands to bless the people and the glory of the Lord appeared to confirm that the sacrifices had been received. 'And when all the people saw it,' we read, 'they shouted for joy and fell face down' (Lev. 9:24).

But the process began with Moses saying to Aaron: 'Come to the altar and sacrifice your sin offering and your burnt offering and make atonement for yourself and the people' (Lev. 9:7). Only once Aaron had sacrificed for his sins could he bring 'the offering that was for the people' (Lev. 9:15).

This need for a priest to offer a sacrifice for his own sins is a bit of a giveaway. It shows that the priests are just as sinful as the people they serve. They need atonement just as much as anyone else. They're as needy as we are.

But Jesus is a high priest who 'truly meets our need – one who is holy, blameless, pure, set apart from sinners, exalted above the heavens' (v. 26). As a result: 'Unlike the other high priests, he does not need to offer sacrifices day after day, first for his own sins, and then for the sins of the people. He sacrificed for their sins once for all when he offered himself' (v. 27). There are two contrasts here. First, the old priests sacrificed 'day after day' while Jesus sacrificed 'once for all'. Second, the old priests sacrificed 'first for his own sins' while Jesus only sacrificed 'for their sins'.

Jesus is the perfect priest offering the perfect sacrifice. 'For the law appoints as high priests men in all their weakness; but the oath, which came after the law, appointed the Son, who has been made perfect for ever' (v. 28). Weak priests have been replaced by a perfect priest; and temporary priests have been replaced by a permanent priest.

Reflection

'For we do not have a high priest who is unable to feel sympathy for our weaknesses, but we have one who has been tempted in every way, just as we are – yet he did not sin' (4:15). Because Jesus was tempted he can empathise with your weaknesses. Because he did not sin he can cleanse your guilt forever.

The punchline to this chapter is the word 'Son' in verse 28. This is the big reveal. This perfect, permanent priest is none other than 'the Son'.

It's a term that Hebrews has kept using for Jesus. In many ways, the first half of the letter is an extended description of 'the Son'. So we're meant to go, 'Who has God appointed as my priest? He's appointed the Son. Who's the Son? Oh yes, I remember... The Son is God's final word to humanity (1:1–2). The Son is the heir of all things (1:2). The Son is the one through whom God made the universe (1:2). The Son is the radiance of God's glory and the exact representation of his being (1:3). The Son is the one who sustains all things by his powerful word (1:3). The Son is the one who is seated at the right hand of God (1:3). The Son is the one who is superior to the angels (1:4). The Son is the one who has been adopted as king by God (1:5). The Son is the one whose throne will last forever (1:8). The Son is the faithful one who is over God's house (3:6). The Son is the one who has ascended into heaven (4:14). The Son is the one who has been made perfect through suffering (5:8–9). The Son is the source of eternal salvation (5:9).'

This is the one who has been appointed as *your* priest. Say it to yourself now: 'Who is my priest? The Son is my priest.' Look again at those descriptions of the Son and say, 'That's my priest.'

So what do we have to do in the light of the perfect priesthood of the Son? Answer: Nothing. There is literally no command in this chapter – not a single one. All the action is done by Christ. There's nothing left for you to do.

The writer does make one exhortation several chapters later in Hebrews 10:21–22: 'since we have a great priest over the house of God, *let us draw near to God* with a sincere heart and with the full assurance that faith brings'. Don't let your sin stop you coming to God – whether for the first time as a new Christian or for the 100th time as a guilty, troubled Christian. Don't let the specific sin that weighs on your mind stop you coming. For Jesus is a perfect priest with an indestructible life who is able to save completely.

Reflection

Right now the Son is interceding for you. Hear him plead your case. Hear him speak on your behalf. See him at the Father's side. Fix your eyes upon Jesus. And come without fear, without shame and without hesitation.

Chapter 3

Jesus is the Covenant Mediator (Hebrews 8)

An upgraded priest Hebrews 8:1–6

In Hebrews 7 we saw that Jesus is a *better priest* because he doesn't have to offer sacrifices for his own sin and because he lives forever.

But while these might prove Jesus is *better*, they don't actually prove that he's a *priest!* After all, Jesus never really looked like a priest. There were only a few occasions when he entered the temple and there's no indication he ever got beyond the outer courtyard. As a non-Levite he wouldn't have been allowed in the temple itself. Plus he never offered an animal sacrifice. Jesus was accused of many things, but no-one thought to call him a priest (or a fake priest). So how can the writer claim Jesus is our priest?

Think about what a priest does: a priest enters a sanctuary and offers a sacrifice. So if Jesus is a true priest he must enter a sanctuary and offer a sacrifice. And that's exactly what the writer says.

- *Jesus enters a sanctuary* (v. 2). The sanctuary Jesus enters is in heaven. (The writer is going to spend chapter 9 developing this idea.)

- *Jesus offers a sacrifice* (v. 3). What Jesus offered was himself as a perfect sacrifice. (The writer is going to spend chapter 10 developing this idea.)

It's true Jesus never looked like a priest when he was on earth. That's because he *isn't* a priest on earth. There was no vacancy here on earth; no-one was advertising (v. 4). Even if they had been, Jesus would have been rejected because 'the tribe of Levi' wasn't on his CV.

But Jesus is a priest in heaven serving in a sanctuary in heaven (v. 1–2). And that actually means he's the real thing, because it's the earthly sanctuary that is the 'copy and shadow' (v. 5). So the ministry of Jesus is *'superior'* to anything done on earth (v. 6).

Reflection

When your progress seems slow or you're wondering whether Christianity really works, don't *give* up. Instead *look* up. See your heavenly priest in a heavenly sanctuary.

Perhaps more than any other New Testament letter, the letter of Hebrews emphasises the finished work of the cross. It keeps describing what Jesus did at the cross as 'once for all' (7:27; 9:12, 25–26; 10:10–14).

At the same time the letter of Hebrews – again more than any other New Testament letter – emphasises that *Christ's saving work takes place in heaven.*

The Jewish neighbours of the first readers perhaps taunted them because Christians appear to have no priest, no sacrifice, no sanctuary and no homeland. But the message of Hebrews is that we do in fact have a priest, a sacrifice, a sanctuary and a homeland. Our priest is in heaven (chapter 7), our sanctuary is in heaven (chapter 9), and our homeland is in heaven (chapter 11).

Even our sacrifice, which was offered on earth, is *presented* in heaven. This pattern was prefigured in the work of purification in the old covenant tabernacle. The altar was located *outside* the sanctuary in the courtyard of the tabernacle and this is where sacrifices were offered. The animal was killed and burnt outside the tent. Then its blood was carried *into* the tabernacle and this is where purification took place (especially on the day of atonement). Now Jesus has offered himself on earth (outside the heavenly sanctuary) and then entered heaven on our behalf to make purification for our sins (9:11–12, 24).

So our priest, sacrifice, sanctuary and homeland are *'better'* or *'superior'* – another favourite phrase of the writer of Hebrews.

Verse 1 of chapter 8 says Jesus 'sat down' in heaven (past tense). That's because his work of atonement is done. The price is paid in full. But verse 2 says Jesus 'serves in the sanctuary' (present tense). Jesus is applying the completed work of the cross to our needs as he intercedes on our behalf.

Reflection

Right now Jesus is presenting his finished work before God in heaven on your behalf.

One of my grumpy-old-man complaints is that so-called upgrades often turn out to be worse than what preceded them. I don't want a larger screen on my phone; I want something that fits in my pocket! But the Old Testament covenant was in desperate need of an upgrade and this is what Jesus has provided: 'the ministry Jesus has received is as superior to theirs as the covenant of which he is mediator is superior to the old one, since the new covenant is established on better promises' (v. 6). So thorough is this upgrade that it's left the old covenant obsolete (v. 13).

The whole priestly system operated within a kind of legal framework as part of a contract between God and his people – what the Bible calls a 'covenant'. A covenant is a special kind of legal contract, one that creates a new relationship. The most obvious contemporary example is a marriage covenant. Marriage is a legal agreement that makes a new relationship. On the morning of my wedding day, I was a single man; by the evening, I was a married man. The heart of God's covenant is this: 'I will be their God, and they will be my people' (v. 10). Through this covenant, God and his people entered into a relationship. He became *their* God and they became *his* people.

All the additional covenant regulations made this relationship possible. That's what the sacrifices were for: they made it possible for sinful people to come into the presence of a holy God.

Kind of. They were only a temporary and partial solution. Indeed, their main purpose was to point to Jesus. In and of themselves they couldn't deal with sin. We needed a better priest offering a better sacrifice within a better covenant. 'For if there had been nothing wrong with that first covenant,' says verse 7, 'no place would have been sought for another.'

Reflection

Every now and then a company will send you an email detailing changes in their terms and conditions. They're constantly 'improving' the contract. I'm not sure for whose benefit! In Christ, God has updated his terms and conditions – and the upgrade is all for *our* benefit.

An upgraded promise   Hebrews 8:8-10

To show us how the new covenant is better, the writer of Hebrews turns to the prophet Jeremiah whom he quotes at length. Jeremiah tells us what was wrong with the old covenant.

Did God get it wrong first time round? No, the covenant itself wasn't faulty. The problem was faulty people. 'God found fault with the people,' says verse 8. Why? Because 'they did not remain faithful to my covenant' (v. 9). God made a covenant with his people, but the people couldn't keep it.

So what's the solution? Better promises. 'The new covenant is established on better promises,' says verse 6. And what are those better promises? 'I will put my laws in their minds and write them on their hearts' (v. 10). God remedies the heart of the problem by dealing with the problem of the human heart. God now writes his law on our hearts. On *your* heart.

What does this mean? First, it means God gives us a deeper desire to obey his will.

The problem with the old covenant according to verse 9 was that the people didn't remain faithful. Part of God's solution was *to send Jesus*, to be faithful on our behalf, to live the righteous life that we should have lived, to pay the price we should have paid.

But the other side of his solution was *to send his Spirit* into our hearts, giving us a new desire for obedience, holiness and service.

We're born with a natural tendency to turn in on ourselves in selfishness and pride. When little children are upset or cross, they often curl up into a ball, all tight and tense. There's a sense in which every human being is like this – maybe not on the outside, but on the inside we're tight and tense, curled in on ourselves. But the Spirit begins to warm us with God's love so we open up like a flower. We relax and uncurl. We look up towards God in faith and out towards other people in love.

Reflection

The beginning of true change is not to think first about what we must do, but to think about what God has done – to relax in the warmth of his love to us in Christ.

When I first started preaching, my sermons were all over the place. They were full of random information, all gushing out in a bit of a mess. Fortunately, my mentor introduced me to a sermon template. For years, I used that framework to shape every sermon I preached and it led to a big improvement. But gradually, as I started to get the hang of preaching a bit more, I found I was using the template less. My preaching became a bit more intuitive.

In one sense, God's law has always been short and simple: love God and love other people. But at first God had to spell out what this meant in a host of different situations. 'In this scenario you do this… In that scenario you do that.' That's what the written law of Moses did. It provided a template for obedience.

But now God has written his law on our hearts (v. 10). It's not that we're free to do whatever we want – we're still bound to love God and other people. But now we have a more instinctive grasp of God's will. We're better at working out what to do in new scenarios – scenarios not anticipated in any set of regulations.

The law on our hearts also goes beyond mere actions. Now we keep the letter and spirit of the law. Suppose your son hits his sister. So you tell him to say sorry. 'Sorry,' he says in a whiny tone. Has he obeyed you? Not really. There's no regret or remorse. But you can't create a law to impose remorse. According to the letter of your law he's done the right thing: he's said the word 'sorry'. But it's empty obedience. The law written on our hearts means *we obey from the heart*.

This doesn't mean we can dispense with the Bible. In an age of moral relativism, we need the guidance of Scripture more than ever.

It's all too easy to claim we're being prompted by the Spirit when we're really following our own desires. The Spirit doesn't replace the Bible with some subjective inner sense of morality. Quite the opposite. The Spirit teaches us God's ways from God's word so they become embedded in our hearts. But we don't rely merely on proof texts. Instead, the Spirit uses the Bible as a whole to reshape our moral compass and supercharge our conscience.

Reflection

What's shaping your moral instincts? God's word or the values of this world?

The new covenant is better because God writes his laws on our hearts, giving us a new motivation for obedience and new understanding of his will. But the blessing of the new covenant goes much, much further. Verse 11 says:

> No longer will they teach their neighbours,
>   or say to one another, 'Know the Lord,'
> because they will all know me,
>   from the least of them to the greatest.

The point is not that we can't benefit from preachers or learn from one another. The point is we don't need other people to *mediate* for us. We can all know God for ourselves in a relational sense.

Every sermon, every song, every Bible study, every word of encouragement is part of that process of God writing his law on your heart. But it's far more than information. We're coming to know God in a personal way. Indeed, it's the personal knowledge of God that drives our deepening desire to obey God's will and our growing instinct for knowing what his will is.

Think about a company director who hires a PA. At first, the director has to tell the PA exactly how they want things done. But gradually the PA gets to know the director and starts to anticipate what they want. That's partly what's going on as God writes his law on our hearts. God himself in the person of his Spirit is imprinting these things on your mind and impressing them on your hearts. Now think of a man who marries a woman. He proves to be a good, thoughtful, loving husband. So her love for him grows and grows.

She not only *knows* how she can please him, she *wants* to show her love and please him. Her heart is full of love so she's keen to serve the one who has loved her so well.

That's what it means to grow as a Christian. Yes, we have a growing understanding of God's will. But what really fuels our obedience is a growing grasp of his love.

Reflection

Fix your eyes on Jesus. Jesus displays God's will so looking at Jesus makes our understanding of God's will more instinctive. And Jesus displays God's love so looking at Jesus makes our motivation to obey grow stronger.

I think my memory is getting worse as I get older. Or perhaps it's just that I'm no longer quick-witted enough to cover up when I forget someone's name.

What about God's memory? Surely God doesn't forget. No, he doesn't. Indeed, since God is eternal and therefore outside of time, it may be that every moment in time is always present to him.

And yet, here in verse 12, Jeremiah (and now the writer of Hebrews) tells us that there is something God does not remember – our sins:

> For I will forgive their wickedness
>   and will remember their sins no more.

It's not that God fails to recollect them. In the Bible 'remembering' is a covenantal term. That means remembering is really another way of talking about keeping covenant promises. To remember a promise is to keep a promise. God no longer remembers our sin because he has promised to forgive our wickedness. Our sin has been dealt with through the new covenant. Christ has paid the price and so God no longer factors our sins into the way he treats us.

If you're a Christian and you're feeling guilty then your problem is this: you're better at remembering your sin than God is. If you go to God and say, 'You know that thing I did that haunts me, that guilt that feels like it's crushing me…' God replies, 'I don't know what you're talking about. I don't remember. All I remember is the sacrifice of my Son. All I remember is his blood dripping from his hands and feet. All I remember is his desperate cry that I could not answer. I remember that. But I don't remember your sin.'

When he gave us the Lord's Supper, Jesus said: 'This is my blood of the covenant, which is poured out for many for the forgiveness of sins' (Mt. 26:28). This is the new covenant promised by Jeremiah. At its heart is the promise of forgiveness. And that promise is renewed every time we take bread and wine.

Reflection

As we remember the death of Christ in communion, God is forgetting our sins.

Chapter 4

Jesus is the Complete Sacrifice (Hebrews 9)

I once noticed a smell in our house. I caught a whiff of something wrong, but I couldn't work out what it was. It was still there the following day. We searched the house but found nothing. Eventually behind the piano we found a dead bird that our cat had brought in. For days afterwards, we were spraying air-freshener and apologising to guests. Nobody wants to visit a stinky home.

The drain in our old house would periodically get blocked. A little pool of dishwater would emerge outside the back door. And it was my job to sort it. I bought the thickest rubber gloves I could find. But even then my hands would smell horribly afterwards. I'd wash them in soap. Then with washing-up liquid. Then with soap again. But they would still smell.

Nobody wants to visit a stinky home and nobody wants to hang out with a stinky person.

What about your heart? What about the stench of your sin? How do you clean that up?

Where can we find a clean place to meet God and how can we be clean enough to meet him there? Those are the questions addressed in Hebrews 9.

The writer begins by reminding us what the old covenant tabernacle was like. It was a mixture of promise and problem. It encapsulated the *problem* posed by God's holiness and our sin. The curtain kept us from the Most Holy Place (v. 3) and the day of atonement showed the need for cleansing (v. 7). 'The Holy Spirit was showing by this,' says verse 8, 'that the way into the Most Holy

Place had not yet been disclosed as long as the first tabernacle was still functioning.'

In the meantime, the tabernacle also embodied the *promise* of intimacy with God. It was a place where people can meet God and eat a meal with him – represented by the consecrated bread in verse 2.

Reflection

How is the promise of a meal with God fulfilled in the present? How will it be fulfilled in the future?

Imagine you're building a new house. If I ask you, 'What's it going to look like?' then you'll show me the architect's model. Let's move on several months. Now the house has been built and you've moved in. What happens now if I ask, 'What's it look like?' You're not going to show me the architect's model. That's become, as the writer of Hebrews puts it, 'obsolete' (8:13). Instead you'll say, 'Come inside and I'll show you round.'

The tabernacle was an architect's model – a picture of what God would do. 'This is an illustration for the present time,' says verse 9. But we mustn't confuse the model with the real thing. The tabernacle is not the way to God. It was 'not able to clear the conscience of the worshipper' (v. 9). It couldn't remove the stench of sin.

The first readers of Hebrews were Jewish Christians and we can imagine their neighbours saying, 'We've got the temple. What have you got? Nothing.' So Hebrews reminds them that the earthly temple was just a temporary illustration. It embodied the promise of a meal with God, but it couldn't deliver that promise. It couldn't remove the stain and stench of sin. It only 'worked' by evoking faith in what was *coming* – the fulfilment of the promise and the solution to the problem.

But now Christ has entered 'the *greater and more perfect* tabernacle that is not made with human hands, that is to say, is not a part of this creation' (v. 11). It's a 'greater' sanctuary because (a) it's not made by human hands – it's made by God; and (b) it's not part of this (visible) creation – it's in heaven.

The ark in the tabernacle was built like a footstool. God sat enthroned in heaven, but his footstool was in the tabernacle – a sign that his reign reached down to earth. But Jesus has come before the actual throne of God in heaven. He has come into God's presence.

Reflection

You and I have not yet reached the heavenly sanctuary. But we're not left homeless in the meantime. Describing the church, Ephesians 2:21–22 says: 'In him the whole building is joined together and rises to become a holy temple in the Lord. And in him you too are being built together to become a dwelling in which God lives by his Spirit.' When you meet with God's people you're meeting in the place where God dwells!

We had some workmen in recently who started installing a stove, but they had to leave the job half done because they lacked the parts they needed. Jesus has come and gone and will come a second time. But that's not because he left the job of atoning for sin half done. When we fix our eyes on Jesus we see not only a greater sanctuary, but also a better sacrifice (v. 23).

The blood of animal sacrifices produced a kind of outward ceremonial purity (v. 13). 'How much more, then,' says verse 14, 'will the blood of Christ, who through the eternal Spirit offered himself unblemished to God, cleanse our consciences from acts that lead to death, so that we may serve the living God!' This sacrifice is better because this sacrifice is Jesus himself. By 'his own blood,' says verse 12. 'Christ … offered himself,' says verse 14. The God-man offered himself. He was an 'unblemished' sacrifice (v. 14). The only person who did not deserve to die offered himself to die in our place. The one who was full of life – with an 'indestructible life' (as 7:16 puts it) – died for us so that his life might burst into our lives.

Jesus is a better sacrifice and as a result he has obtained 'eternal redemption' (v. 12). One reason we can be sure the sacrifice of Jesus created eternal redemption is because Jesus only did it once. The sacrifice offered on the day of atonement was offered every year, over and over again (v. 25). It had to be repeated because last year's had, as it were, worn off. But the sacrifice of Jesus has been offered 'once for all' (v. 26). The sacrifice of Jesus creates eternal redemption because it's complete. It covers every sin – past, present and future. There will never be a need to repeat it.

There is still one stage left in the story of salvation. We're still waiting for Jesus to 'appear a second time' (v. 28). But Jesus is not coming again 'to bear sin' – that work is finished because sin has been taken away (v. 28). All that's left is for Jesus to restore God's rule and renew all things.

Reflection

Christ will appear a second time. In the meantime, what are Christians doing according to verse 28? And what are we to do according to verse 14?

Not only does Jesus create an eternal redemption, he also brings an eternal inheritance. 'For this reason Christ is the mediator of a new covenant,' says verse 15, 'that those who are called may receive the promised eternal inheritance – now that he has died as a ransom to set them free from the sins committed under the first covenant.'

Under the old covenant, God's people were required to keep God's law. But they failed. And under the terms of the covenant that meant they faced the penalty of death and there was no escape. But Christ has freed us from the penalty of death by dying in our place. He has paid the ransom price and so set us free from the terms of the old covenant. But not only are we set free from the *old* covenant, we're also brought into a *new* covenant – a new contract or deal. It's a contract in which we receive the promised eternal inheritance – a place in heaven.

So how do we move from the old covenant to the new covenant?

First, the death of Jesus *ends the old covenant* (v. 16–17). A covenant is a bit like a will and you can't claim your inheritance until someone has died! In a similar way, the old covenant promised an inheritance (v. 15), but we couldn't receive that inheritance until someone had died – the person of Christ on behalf of the triune God. Now the will can be read and we can receive an inheritance.

Second, the death of Jesus *begins the new covenant* (v. 18–20). The first covenant was put into effect through blood (Ex. 24:1–8). Shedding blood was like shaking hands on a deal or signing the bottom of a contract. 'This is the blood of the covenant,' Moses said (v. 20). They're words echoed by Jesus at the Last Supper: 'This is my blood of the covenant, which is poured out for many for the forgiveness of sins' (Mt. 26:28).

Reflection

You can say, 'Heaven belongs to me. There's a little bit of God's new creation with my name on it.'

Imagine the Queen is coming to your house for a meal. My hunch is you would hurry home, tidy up and give everywhere a good clean. Now imagine you're going to eat a meal in the presence of *God*. What are you going to do? You're going to make sure the place where you meet is clean. Where is that? The greater sanctuary – the sanctuary in heaven.

In the past, coal fires created a deep, dense smog in British cities. At times you could hardly see across the road. As a result most buildings were black with soot. My in-laws smoked for most of their lives. Their ceilings were yellow with the stain of the smoke. Whenever we came home after visiting them we would open our suitcases to be greeted by the smell of stale smoke. The same kind of thing is going on with *God's* house. Like smog in a city or cigarette smoke in a house, our sin and death have polluted God's sanctuary.

At this point you might be thinking, 'How do we pollute God's sanctuary if it's in heaven?' The same question might be asked of the earthly tabernacle. The book of Leviticus describes an extensive system of cleanliness and purity – all designed to keep the Most Holy Place free from pollution. But even with these protective regulations, the germs and smells of human sin were gradually deposited on God's house. So the Most Holy Place needed an annual spring clean and that's what took place on the day of atonement (Lev. 16). The day of atonement did two things: it cleansed the *people's sin*, but it also cleansed *God's sanctuary*. Sacrificial blood was like a spiritual detergent that removed the stain of sin and the stench of death.

In the same way, the stench of sin and death have pervaded God's sanctuary in heaven. Our sin has created a kind of cosmic pollution that needs to be cleansed. It will certainly be there when we arrive, open our suitcases and release the stale smell of sin and death.

But Jesus has cleansed the heavenly sanctuary through his blood (v. 23). And it's not just an annual spring clean. It's a once-for-all clean up.

Reflection

The blood of Jesus is a powerful detergent that wipes away the stain and stench of sin.

In Sheffield (where I used to live) coal dust was often used in old plasterwork. So any major house renovation involved thick clouds of soot. Everyone and everything would get covered in black dust. Imagine getting filthy after a day's work on your house. You'll have a shower and put on clean clothes. But what about the house? If you're having friends over for a meal, it's no good you being clean if there's a thick layer of soot on the table, the chairs and the food!

The pollution of our sin has created a cloud of smog and soot. Humanity's sin doesn't just affect humanity. It's infected the whole of the cosmos. Creation has been 'subjected to frustration' and is in 'bondage to decay' (Rom. 8:20–21). The stain of our sin is found everywhere – in every sign of decay, pollution, stench and death.

There was a time when God would walk with humanity in the cool of the evening. But the world is no longer a fit place for God's presence.

Under the old covenant, God, as it were, carved out a little bit of clean space where he could dwell. That's what the Most Holy Place represented. But even the Most Holy Place needed to keep being cleansed – hence the spring clean on the day of atonement.

That was a picture of what Jesus would do. For Jesus has now cleaned up heaven (as we saw yesterday).

And one day he's going to 'bring salvation' to us (v. 28). One day, heaven and earth will be united in a world made new and God will again dwell among his people (Rev. 21:1–5). The coming new creation is going to be a temple-garden. And Hebrews 9 says it has been cleansed by the blood of Jesus from the stain of sin so that it can again be a place where we can walk with God.

Reflection

Jesus has created a place where we can meet with God.

A world-made-new is for the future. In the meantime, the sacrifice of Jesus has not only cleansed a *place* so we can meet God. It's also cleansed a *people* who can meet with God. It's cleansed *you* if you're a Christian! 'How much more, then,' says verse 14, 'will the blood of Christ, who through the eternal Spirit offered himself unblemished to God, cleanse our consciences from acts that lead to death, so that we may serve the living God!'

Verse 13 combines two old covenant acts of cleansing: the cleansing from sin on the day of atonement (Lev. 16) and the cleansing from death after contact with a dead body (Num. 19). We're cleansed both from our sin and from the decay it has brought to our lives.

Remember my hands smelling of drains? I used to worry that people would think I was stinky. Do you fear people will catch a whiff of your sin? Is there a particular sin that tugs at your conscience? Perhaps there's something you still replay in your mind. Or perhaps there's a sinful habit that you've done again and again. What's the skeleton in your closet? What's the weight you carry in your heart?

The blood of Jesus has cleansed you of *that* sin. Not just sin in general, but *that* sin, that bad smell that lingers round your soul.

The blood of Jesus is a powerful, spiritual detergent that washes us clean. Jesus 'offered himself unblemished' (v. 14). And now before God we're *unblemished* – just like Jesus. At the cross, God put your dirty, stinking soul into the washing machine and washed it clean with the blood of Jesus.

That means that one day you'll be able to walk with God in the new creation temple-garden. Even now we can come to God with 'confidence' with 'our hearts sprinkled to cleanse us from a guilty conscience' (10:19, 22).

Reflection

What only the high priest could do, and what he could do only once a year, you can do every moment of every day.

Chapter 5

Jesus is the Living Way
(Hebrews 10)

In 1984, peat cutters in Cheshire found the remains of a man in Lindow bog. It turns out the body was 2,000 years old. The man had been strangled, hit on the head and his throat had been cut. It was almost certainly a ritual sacrifice.

The practice of sacrifice is remarkably prevalent across the world. In most cultures of the world, people have offered sacrifices; often animal sacrifices, sometimes even human sacrifices. Why is this practice widespread in such dispersed cultures? Maybe it's because we have an intuitive sense that something must die that we might live. Maybe it's an echo – albeit sometimes a horribly distorted echo – of an original divine command to the first man and woman.

Sacrifice still pervades our culture. Athletes make sacrifices to secure victory. You may not be a medal prospect, but you may make sacrifices to get a body you can be proud off – sacrificing a second helping or time in bed. People make sacrifices to get an education or progress in their career. And people sometimes still sacrifice their children in pursuit of success or pleasure. Or maybe you're trying to cure your guilt, so you attempt to atone by harming yourself.

Your god is the thing (or person) you want most or whatever you can't live without. So to get it or keep it you make sacrifices. You sacrifice to your god. We're all at it.

But it doesn't work. That's the sobering message of verses 1–4. The argument is simple. A moment's thought shows us that sacrifices never make us perfect. If they did, we would stop doing them. If you think your trips to the gym or your extra hours at work or the scratches on your wrist are solving your problems, then ask yourself this: can you stop? You try to appease your god, but its demands are relentless. Pain may relieve pain, but only for a moment. Nothing you do cleanses you on the inside.

Reflection

In what ways do you make sacrifices? What's the effect of those sacrifices in your life?

In verses 5–7, the writer of Hebrews says that God never wanted sacrifices. Now that's an astonishing claim. For hundreds of years, people all over the world have been offering sacrifices on the assumption they were giving God what he wanted! Wasn't it God who invented sacrifice? After all, sacrifice was part of his law (v. 8)?

The point is this: sacrifice was never for God's benefit. What could it do for him? What does the God of heaven want with a dead cow?

No, sacrifices were given for *our* benefit. They were given as a dramatic visual aid to show us two things: (a) the seriousness of sin, and (b) the solution for sin.

First, God gave us sacrifices to show us the *seriousness* of sin: 'those sacrifices are an annual reminder of sins,' says verse 3. The squeals of the animal, the blood dropping to the floor, the smell of burning flesh are all designed to show us the terrible consequences of sin. The temple in Israel was not like a cathedral. It was like an abattoir.

Second, God gave us sacrifices to point to the *solution* for sin. Think about how a sacrifice works. Something is lost so that something else might be gained. Something dies so that something else might live. Sacrifice is about replacement or substitution. My sin should lead to my death. But with a sacrifice there is a replacement or substitution. With an animal sacrifice, I am symbolically replaced by the animal. A sheep or cow dies in my place.

But animal sacrifices were a pointer to Jesus. 'He sets aside the first to establish the second,' says verse 9. The 'first' here is the sacrifice of animals. The 'second' is the sacrifice of Jesus. With the death of Jesus, symbolism becomes reality. Jesus died in my place. He took the punishment I deserve. So I am free from the consequences of sin.

Reflection

God doesn't *demand* sacrifices – because God *gives* the sacrifice. Jesus the Son of God says, 'Here I am ... I have come to do your will.'

Are you feeling weary? However much you do, it's never enough. All your efforts are not enough for you to feel like a good person or win people's approval. Perhaps it feels like they're not enough for God.

Jesus is our high priest. Hebrews has already established that in chapters 7–8. But Jesus is also the sacrifice: 'He sacrificed for their sins once for all when he offered himself' (7:27). Jesus is our priest and Jesus is the sacrifice.

And the sacrifice of Jesus works. The key verse in chapter 10 is verse 10: 'we have been made holy through the sacrifice of the body of Jesus Christ once for all'. If the test of whether a sacrifice really works is whether it has to be repeated then the sacrifice of Jesus has clearly worked. It was once for all. It has never been repeated. It will never need to be repeated. The job is done.

'Day after day every priest stands and performs his religious duties,' says verse 11, 'again and again he offers the same sacrifices, which can never take away sins.' Day after day. Again and again. I wonder if that describes you. You overwork day after day, again and again. You push yourself day after day, again and again. You try to please others day after day, again and again. But however much you do, it's never enough.

'But when this priest had offered for all time one sacrifice for sins, he sat down' (v. 12).

- 'For all time.' This really is never again.

- 'One sacrifice.' There's no need for you to sacrifice.

- 'He sat down.' He's not on his feet because his work is done.

And, it's time for you to sit down. For Jesus has made you perfect 'for ever' (v. 14).

Reflection

It's right for us to work hard to serve God. But if you're chasing success or love or approval or forgiveness or self-esteem, you'll always be running and you'll always be weary. Meanwhile, God is saying: Stop! Because atonement has been made.

Forget because God has forgotten Hebrews 10:15–18

Once when I was a teenager I helped myself to a piece of chocolate at a friend's house. When he realised, he said in a sarcastic voice, 'Why don't you have a piece of my chocolate?' I'd been caught and exposed. But, for some strange reason that has eluded me ever since, I decided to brazen my way out of the situation by taking his words at face value. So I took another piece! I've remembered that moment over and over again with shame. And that's just an example of a regret I'm prepared to tell you about!

I wonder whether your past haunts you: some deep guilt you can't erase or a profound sense of shame you can't shake off. Today the Holy Spirit himself has something to tell us (v. 15): '"Their sins and lawless acts I will remember no more." And where these have been forgiven, sacrifice for sin is no longer necessary' (v. 17–18).

God says to us: 'I will remember no more.' My friend Ben told me once how he lent £200 to a friend. Every time he saw his friend, Ben couldn't help thinking of the £200 with resentment. Perhaps it affected his friend too, filling him with guilt. 'It ruined our friendship,' Ben told me. Things only changed when Ben forgave the debt. After that the relationship was restored. Of course Ben had to pay a price for that reconciliation – he had to forego his £200.

So it is with God. The debt we owe to God ruins our relationship. But God has forgiven our debt, paying the price himself with the blood of his Son. As a result, the debt is forgotten and the relationship is restored.

You don't have to live in the past. Your guilt need not determine your future. You can be set free by the sacrifice of Christ. Maybe your sin messed up a relationship. It could mess up your next relationship. But it doesn't have to. You can bring your sin to the cross of Christ. Or maybe your sin weighs heavily on your heart. Maybe you self-harm to make amends. Maybe you think of yourself as a bad person who deserves bad things. The cross sets you free.

Reflection

Today the Holy Spirit is testifying to *you*: 'where these have been forgiven, sacrifice for sin is no longer necessary' (v. 18).

I wonder if you feel dirty. Maybe it is the shame of what you've done. Maybe it's the shame of what others have done to you.

The writer of Hebrews addresses people who feel dirty inside. He says 'let us draw near to God with a sincere heart and with the full assurance that faith brings, having our hearts sprinkled to cleanse us from a guilty conscience and having our bodies washed with pure water' (v. 22).

The imagery is taken from the Old Testament temple. People could only enter the temple if they were sprinkled with the blood of sacrifice. It was a sign that we need cleansing if we're to come to God because he is pure and holy. But now through the blood of Jesus we can draw near to God with full assurance, with cleansed hearts, with washed bodies.

At the centre of the temple was the Most Holy Place. It symbolised the presence of God. So there was a thick curtain to stop people entering. But at the very moment at which Jesus died that curtain was torn in two. So now there is 'a new and living way opened for us through the curtain' (v. 20). The body of Jesus crucified for us is that 'new and living way'. He died to cleanse us. He rose to become a living way. And he ascended to lead us back into God's presence.

Reflection

Meditate on this hymn by Joseph Hart:

Come, ye sinners, poor and needy,
weak and wounded, sick and sore.
Jesus ready stands to save you,
full of pity, love and pow'r.
He is able, he is willing, doubt no more.

Come, ye weary, heavy-laden,
lost and ruined by the Fall.
If you wait until you're better
you will never come at all.
Not the righteous, sinners Jesus came to call.

Perhaps you've been plugging away faithfully as a Christian – serving in your church, helping those in need, sharing your faith with unbelievers, raising your family as best you can, volunteering in your neighbourhood. But progress is slow. Growth is slow. Evangelism is hard work. Family life is messy.

We've seen that Jesus is a better priest (chapter 7) and the mediator of a better covenant (chapter 8), who enters a better sanctuary (chapter 9) through a better sacrifice (chapter 10). The application of all this comes in verses 19–25. 'Let us' the writer says three times over. The first we've met already: 'let us draw near' (v. 22). Now we meet two more:

- 'Let us hold unswervingly to the hope we profess' (v. 23).

- 'And let us consider how we may spur one another on' (v. 24).

They go together. The first is a call to *keep going* as a Christian. The second is a call to *keep meeting* – to let other Christians help us keep going. It's also a call to help other Christians keep going.

The writer follows up these exhortations with another strong warning (v. 26–27). If you reject Christ then there's no alternative. There's no other sacrifice for sin. There's no other way to God. It was bad enough when people rejected God's word when it came through Moses; how much worse will it be if people reject God's word in Jesus (v. 28–31).

How do we keep going? Top of the to-do-list is this: by 'not giving up meeting together' (v. 25). It's by coming together as a church week-by-week that *I* will keep going and that I can help *you* keep going.

Reflection

Verse 24 does not simply say, 'let us spur one another on'. It goes a bit further. It's a call to *'consider'* how we might spur one another on – to think of the best way we can encourage one another. So take a moment to consider who you could encourage and how.

If you're feeling weary or losing heart then the writer of Hebrews has a message for you. What these verses tell us (along with the following chapter) is this: *it's worth it!*

The writer has just warned us about the terrible dangers of falling away (v. 26–31). But that's not the trajectory the readers of Hebrews are on. Instead, the writer reminds them of how far they've already come. 'Remember those earlier days after you had received the light,' he says in verse 32, 'when you endured in a great conflict full of suffering.' He lists some of their sufferings: insult, persecution, imprisonment, confiscation. 'So do not throw away your confidence; it will be richly rewarded' (v. 35).

How can you keep going when it's tough? There are some answers in these verses. Verse 34 says, 'You suffered along with those in prison and joyfully accepted the confiscation of your property, *because you knew that you yourselves had better and lasting possessions.*' What are those better possessions? Well, we've met the word 'better' several times already in Hebrews. The writer talks about how Jesus has a better name and offers a better promise, a better hope, a better covenant, a better sacrifice. The better possessions are the better future promised to us in Christ.

'You need to persevere so that when you have done the will of God,' says verse 36, 'you will receive what he has promised.' Again the writer is pointing us forward. And his message is: it's worth it. How do we keep going when it's tough? *By looking forward.* We look forward to the better future that God has promised.

Reflection

Often spiritual growth can feel painfully slow. We're all too aware of our sin or the weakness of our church. But take a moment to look back over the past year or the past few years. Can you see how far God has brought you? Can you see how he's kept you through difficult times? Can you see how he's used those difficulties to make you more like Jesus?

Chapter 6

Jesus is the Ultimate Pioneer (Hebrews 11:1–12:17)

'Now faith is confidence in what we hope for and assurance about what we do not see,' says verse 1. There are other good ways of defining 'faith'. But the focus here for the writer of Hebrews is on the way *faith looks forwards*. Faith is trusting God's promises and a promise is, by definition, a word about the future. We're trusting that what God has said about the future will happen. And we're staking our lives on those promises.

Suppose someone were to send you an email that says: 'If you sell up, cash in all your savings and buy a ticket to Australia, then I will give you an island paradise.' What do you do? It all depends on whether you trust them! Because you're going to be staking a lot on their word. If you can't trust them then you'll mark their email as spam and delete it. But if you can trust them, then you'll act in a completely different way. You'll make big sacrifices because you're confident it will be worth it.

What about the readers of this letter? What about us? We're staking a lot. We're risking insult, persecution, imprisonment, confiscation (10:33–35). Whether you think it will be worth it depends on whether you think the promise of God can be trusted.

Back in 10:35 the writer said: 'So do not throw away your confidence; it will be richly rewarded.' Here in verse 6 he repeats the same message: 'And without faith it is impossible to please God, because anyone who comes to him must believe that he exists and that he rewards those who earnestly seek him.' If we're to keep going we need be sure that God rewards those who keep going. We need to be sure that it's worth it. We need to be sure God can be trusted.

So the rest of chapter 11 is a series of case studies that all prove this point. We'll focus on three of those case studies: Abraham, Moses and Jesus himself.

Reflection

We keep going by looking forward to the better future that God has promised.

I love planning; I like to know what I'm doing. Abraham gave all that up. He obeyed 'even though he did not know where he was going' (v. 8). Abraham gave up certainty. He also gave up a sense of belonging to live 'like a stranger' (v. 9). The Bible talks about how Christians are strangers in this world; we used to fit in, but now we have different priorities. Abraham also gave up his home and 'lived in tents,' says verse 9. Why did he do it? 'For he was looking forward to the city with foundations, whose architect and builder is God' (v. 10). He gave up a home on earth because he was looking forward to a homeland in heaven (v. 16). It was worth it because Abraham was heading for something *better*.

Here's the key thing: like Abraham, Sarah acted in faith 'because she considered him faithful who had made the promise' (v. 11). It's only worth leaving behind your old way of life as Abraham did if you can be sure your future life will be better. It's only worth enduring suffering, as the readers of Hebrews are doing, if you can be sure God will deliver. Can we trust the promise? Yes, because we can trust *the Promise-Maker*. God is faithful. He doesn't lie. He doesn't play games with us. He has a 100 per cent track record of delivering on his promises.

When we think about homemaking we might think of mortgages, curtains, colour charts and furniture. They're an inevitable part of our lives. But our true home is in heaven. The home-making that counts is to store up treasure in heaven (Mt. 6:19–21). It's only by looking ahead to our true home that we can view our earthly home in the right perspective.

If our eyes drop from the heavenly horizon then the things of earth quickly become too important. We start to worry about our financial security. Or we start to obsess about our decor. Or we start to envy what other people have. What's the solution? Lift your eyes. Look ahead to a better home in a better country.

Reflection

Perhaps you need to stop reading lifestyle magazines and browsing social media for craft ideas, and spend more time meditating on the promises of God in his word.

I love going to the British Museum. You can reach out to touch objects from Bible times – or at least you could if they weren't protected in glass cases. It feels as if the Bible story is there before you. You can see papyri from New Testament times, statues from Assyria and gold-plated sarcophagi from ancient Egypt.

The Egyptian rulers were very wealthy. They had the equivalent of today's multi-millionaire lifestyles. And that was the life Moses enjoyed. For he was raised as a member of the royal court. So Moses had it all. He could have anything and do anything.

But Moses gave it all up. In fact, not only did he give it all up, he chose to be ill-treated (v. 25). He chose to side with God's people even though they were slaves. He chose God, even though that meant choosing disgrace (v. 26).

Why? 'Because he was looking ahead to his reward' (v. 26). Moses wasn't living for this life. He chose to live in the light of the promises of God.

The Egyptians locked up their treasures in the pyramids so they could take them into the afterlife. But they couldn't. How do I know? Because I've seen their treasures in the British Museum.

Moses made a calculation. He looked at all the vast treasures of Egypt that were there for him to enjoy. And he looked at the reward of knowing Christ – a reward which he couldn't see and couldn't touch. 'He regarded disgrace for the sake of Christ as of *greater value* than the treasures of Egypt, because he was looking ahead to his reward' (v. 26). He did the maths. He worked out which was worth more and which would last longer. And so he chose Christ.

Reflection

What might it mean for you to do the maths today? Weigh up the value of the worldly ambitions you harbour or the earthly treasures you covet or the selfish desires you entertain. What are they worth? What will they be worth to you in 100 years' time? And then consider what 'the sake of Christ' means and consider the 'reward' that God promises. What is Christ worth to you?

There's one final case study that we can't ignore:

> *Therefore, since we are surrounded by such a great cloud of witnesses,*
> *let us throw off everything that hinders and the sin that so easily*
> *entangles. And let us run with perseverance the race marked out for*
> *us, fixing our eyes on Jesus, the pioneer and perfecter of faith. For the*
> *joy that was set before him he endured the cross, scorning its shame,*
> *and sat down at the right hand of the throne of God. (v. 1–2)*

The Bible story provides us with a 'cloud of witnesses' (v. 1). We've only had space to look at a couple. The history of the church has added many more stories of people who lived sacrificial lives of service because they were looking forward to the better future that God has promised.

But the ultimate witness is Jesus. We're to fix our eyes on Jesus, 'the pioneer and perfecter of faith' (v. 2).

What did Jesus suffer? The writer highlights two things: Jesus endured the shame of the cross (v. 2) and he endured opposition from sinners (v. 3). I think the writer highlights these things because that's what his readers were enduring. And that may be what you're enduring. People despise you and oppose you because you believe in a crucified Saviour.

So how did Jesus keep going? 'For the joy that was set before him he endured the cross, scorning its shame' (v. 2). Jesus endured the cross because he was looking forward. We keep going by looking forward to the better future that God has promised and it was the same for Jesus. Jesus kept going – even when that meant dying on the cross – because he was looking forward to the better future God had promised.

Reflection

Here's the twist. For Jesus that 'better future' was not his future, but ours. He wasn't doing it for himself; he was doing it for us. But that was his joy! He did it for the joy set before him and *you* are that joy. *You're* the reason Jesus went to the cross.

Christians looking to Jesus   Hebrews 12:1–2

There must be many times during a marathon when you feel like giving up. At least I imagine there must be – I have no first-hand experience of this myself! So why do people keep going? For the satisfaction of finishing. They want to be able to say, 'I did it.' They run 'for the joy set before them'.

The writer of Hebrews says the Christian life is a bit like a marathon: 'let us run with perseverance the race marked out for us,' says verse 1. The goal is not to start the race, but to finish it. And finishing the race requires perseverance.

So how can we keep going to the end?

Answer #1: *We look forward to the better future that God has promised.* Like Abraham, we live as strangers because we're longing for a better home. Like Moses, we reject the pleasures of sin because we're looking ahead to our reward.

Answer #2: *We keep going by 'fixing our eyes on Jesus'* (v. 2). In some ways we're like the saints listed in Hebrews 11. Like them, we've not yet received the reward that we've been promised (11:39). The difference is that we can see Jesus – the pioneer who has gone ahead.

We need to be fixated on Jesus. I wonder what that means for you today? What do you need to *stop* looking at? And what might it mean to fixate on Jesus? Is there some aspect of his character or his work that will keep you going today?

Reflection:

Look to Jesus,
with the look of faith, because our salvation is in Him alone;
with the look of love, because He alone can satisfy our heart;
with the look of strong desire, longing to know Him better;
with the look of soul devotion, waiting only to know His will;
with the look of gladness, because we know He loves us;
with the look of wonder and admiration,
because He is the brightness of the Father's glory, our Lord and
our God.

(from Andrew Murray, *The Holiest of All*, 1894, p. 484)

How do we make sense of hardship in our lives? Here's the answer of Hebrews: 'Endure hardship as discipline; God is treating you as his children' (v. 7).

Imagine a playground full of children. In one corner, you see a small child being told off by an adult man. We wouldn't be surprised to find out that the man is the child's father. Good discipline is a sign of parental love. That's the argument of verses 5–8: 'the Lord disciplines the one he loves' (v. 6). 'God is treating you as his children … true sons and daughters' (v. 7–8). This truth can turn a bad day into a good day! A traffic jam or a work crisis or spilt groceries are all signs of God's love.

Verse 9 begins, 'Moreover'. There's another way of making sense of hardship: God always disciples us for our good (v. 9–10). Most of the time that's what human parents do (although often human discipline gets distorted by our selfishness). But God is a perfect Father and his discipline is unerring. He uses hardship with precision like a skilled sculptor 'in order that we may share in his holiness' (v. 10).

Bad things are still going to be bad. The writer of Hebrews acknowledges that discipline can feel 'painful' (v. 11). Often hardship will remain puzzling to us. We don't have to figure out what God is up to. But we can be confident that God will use adversity to 'produce a harvest of righteousness and peace' (v. 11).

How then should we respond to hardship? 'My son, do not make light of the Lord's discipline,' says verse 5, 'and do not lose heart when he rebukes you.' Instead of making light of it, we're to see hardship as an opportunity to grow. Instead of losing heart, we're to see hardship as a sign of our heavenly Father's love.

This is not something we do on our own. In verses 12–17 the writer gives another exhortation to keep going. But, as we've seen throughout this letter, this comes with a call *to help one another keep going* (v. 15).

Reflection

It's easy to see hardship as a problem to be solved. But Hebrews also encourages us to consider how God might be using it in our lives.

Hebrews 11 is a list of Old Testament heroes. They all model faith that is prepared to put future reward ahead of present pleasures. The ultimate hero is Jesus himself who endured the cross for the joy of seeing his people saved.

At first sight, Hebrews 12 appears to be an abrupt change of direction. Suddenly we're in the middle of a discussion of God's discipline. But these themes are linked by Jesus. Jesus is the supreme example of forward-looking faith. But he's also the supreme example of a Son receiving hardship from his Father.

Jesus is God's Son by nature. As the Nicene Creed says, he is 'of one being with the Father'. Hebrews 1:3 says, 'The Son is the radiance of God's glory and the exact representation of his being'.

But Hebrews 5:8 says, 'Son though he was, he learned obedience from what he suffered'. The divine Son was disciplined. That discipline was not corrective. Instead, God was equipping him to be our high priest, one who is able to sympathise with us in our weakness. Hebrews 12:2 calls Jesus our 'pioneer'. The writer uses the same word in 2:10: 'it was fitting that God … should make the pioneer of their salvation perfect through what he suffered'. Jesus is, as it were, fit for purpose – the purpose of being our high priest. And he is fit for purpose in this way because of the hardship he endured.

Now the writer of Hebrews invites us to 'Consider him' (v. 3). Jesus is our pioneer. He has gone ahead and we now follow in his footsteps. Like Jesus, we are sons and daughters of God – not by nature as Jesus was, but through adoption. Like Jesus, our destination is glory. But like Jesus, the route is marked by suffering. The perfecting of Jesus described in 2:10 and 5:8 becomes our experience in chapter 12. God is perfecting us so we produce a harvest of righteousness and peace.

Reflection

We are one with the Son and therefore loved as sons and daughters by God the Father. Now the Father uses suffering to make us even more like his Son. '... in all things God works for the good of those who love him' that we might 'be conformed to the image of his Son, that [the Son] might be the firstborn among many brothers and sisters' (Rom. 8:28–29).

Chapter 7

Jesus is the Great Shepherd
(Hebrews 12:18–13:25)

Worshipping with angels   Hebrews 12:18–29

Imagine what it was like when God met with his people at Mount Sinai. The writer of Hebrews powerfully evokes the scene in verses 18–21. As you raise your eyes, it looks as if the mountain is on fire. Beneath you the ground is shaking. The summit is enveloped in thick cloud. Your ears hear the sound of a trumpet emerging from the darkness. Then you hear the voice of God booming across the plain on which you stand. You look to Moses for reassurance and find that even he is trembling with fear.

The writer of Hebrews says that something just as amazing takes place every time your church gathers. You enter heaven. Not physically, of course. But through the Holy Spirit, you come to the heavenly Mount Zion. You come before God.

'Therefore, since we have a great high priest who has ascended into heaven,' says Hebrews 4:14–16, '… Let us then approach God's throne of grace with confidence'. Moses ascended through the clouds to the top of Mount Sinai. And now Jesus has ascended through the clouds into heaven. And each Sunday we can join him. We're united to Christ by faith and that means we're with him by faith – with him in the heavenly congregation. 'Therefore, brothers and sisters, since we have confidence to enter the Most Holy Place by the blood of Jesus, by a new and living way … let us draw near to God' (10:19–22).

You may not see fire or hear trumpets. But with the eyes of faith you can worship with the angels. Your song joins their song. They stand among you. When we gather as God's people on earth, we are also gathering with God's people in heaven along with the angels.

The Jewish neighbours of the first readers of Hebrews could worship in Herod's temple. On earth, Christians had no architecture to compete with this. But each Sunday they joined the worship of heaven.

Reflection

The worship in your little church may seem rather tame compared with your favourite Christian worship group or conference – until you remember that you're worshipping with angels!

What's the normal mood when your church gathers for worship?

The mood at Mount Sinai was terror. The people wanted to turn God's voice off (v. 19). Even Moses trembled with fear (v. 21).

But we have come to a 'joyful assembly' (v. 22). Something has changed. It's not God – who continues to be 'a consuming fire' (v. 29). It's not us – for we continue to be born in sin. The difference is Jesus. We have come 'to Jesus the mediator of a new covenant,' says verse 24, 'and to the sprinkled blood that speaks a better word than the blood of Abel'.

Abel was Adam and Eve's second son after Cain. Cain and Abel both came before God with a sacrifice. For reasons that are not entirely clear, God looked with favour on Abel's sacrifice, but not on Cain's. This enraged Cain and, despite a personal warning from God, he murdered his brother. So God said to Cain: 'Listen! Your brother's blood cries out to me from the ground' (Gen 4:10).

Abel's blood represents the blood of all those who have suffered as a result of human sin. If we will listen, then we will hear it crying out for justice. Whenever you suffer unfairly your voice is added to that cry.

But we are also Cain. We are those who have treated others with indifference or cruelty or pride. The blood of Abel cries out against us. God hears that cry and one day justice will be done.

But listen. The blood of Jesus is also crying out and it 'speaks a better word' (v. 24). Abel cries out for justice. The blood of Jesus says justice has been done. On Good Friday, the price of our crimes was paid in full and so now the blood of Jesus speaks a new word: *mercy*. It is that word of mercy that enables us to come before God and join the joyful assembly.

Reflection

Sometimes when we meet, it is right to listen to the cry of the blood of Abel and grieve our sin. But by faith we also hear the cry of the blood of Jesus and rejoice in our forgiveness.

Because of the blood of Jesus, the terror of the assembly at Mount Sinai has been replaced by the joy of the assembly in the heavenly Mount Zion (v. 21–22). But the story of Mount Sinai is not entirely over.

First, *the voice of Mount Sinai still speaks* (v. 25). The voice of God boomed out from Mount Sinai and terrified the people. That voice is still heard today. But now it speaks from heaven. How is that voice heard? It is heard whenever the gospel of Jesus is proclaimed. Your ears may hear a human voice preaching a sermon. But it is God who is speaking to your soul. Or you may be the human voice as you share the gospel with a friend. But God is speaking through you. If we refuse Jesus and his blood then there is no escape from the terror of God's judgment.

Second, *the shaking of Mount Sinai will return* (v. 26–27). At Sinai, the earth shook as God descended on the mountain. The writer of Hebrews (quoting the prophet Haggai) says there's going to be a second shaking. But this will not be local to the Sinai Desert. This time God is going to shake heaven and earth. And only what cannot be shaken will remain.

Imagine a competition in which teams build a tower with straws, paper and tape. The biggest tower wins as long as it can stand under its own strength. Like those towers, one day every human achievement is going to be tested. It's not a test of physical strength, but moral purity. And those who trust in themselves will fall.

But one thing will stand: the kingdom of God (v. 28). Jesus once told the story of two builders. One built his house on sand which fell when the floods came. The other man built his house on rock –

a picture of building your life on the words of Jesus. 'When the flood came, the torrent struck that house but could not shake it, because it was well built' (Lk. 6:48). The word 'shake' is the same word used in Hebrews 12. Those who entrust their lives to Jesus will remain safe in him.

Reflection

We worship God with joy because of the blood of Jesus (v. 22–24). We worship God with reverence because he is a consuming fire (v. 28–29). Does your worship lack joy? Or reverence?

The writer gives six exhortations in the opening verses of chapter 13:

- Keep loving the church family (v. 1).

- Show hospitality to strangers (v. 2).

- Suffer alongside one another (v. 3).

- Honour marriage and remain sexually pure (v. 4).

- Be content with what you have (v. 5).

- Trust your leaders and make their work a joy (v. 7, 17).

This is the church and it's beautiful! Of course, we're not always like this. We're not perfect – not by a long shot. But by the grace of God this is who we are. This chapter doesn't begin: 'Love one another' but '*Keep on* loving one another'. Hebrews 13 is not describing a mythical, utopian or hypothetical community. It's describing a *real* community of *real* Christians. It's describing your local church.

Tucked away in these exhortations are some reasons *why* we can live like this. One is the prospect of entertaining angels unawares (v. 2).

To live a life of love you need to believe in angels! Perhaps that's a bit of a surprise. Why angels? Because angels remind us that we need to see beyond this world. If all we see is what's in front of our eyes then it makes no sense to love others or welcome strangers or suffer alongside those who are ill-treated. These kind of actions will just make you worse off.

But there are angels! And that means there's a world beyond this world and a time beyond this time. And what we do in this world reaches into the heavenly realms and shapes the reward we receive in the next life (or the judgment we receive, v. 4). So everything we do in faith is worth it – if not in this life, then in the next life. This liberates us to live a life of love and create communities of life.

Reflection

Eternity radically changes the maths. *Without* eternity, if you give then you have less. *With* eternity, if you give then you're always left with more!

'Jesus Christ is the same yesterday and today and for ever,' says verse 8. Think what this means. It means the Jesus of yesterday that you read about in the Gospels is the Jesus of today who cares for you right now. And that Jesus is the Jesus of tomorrow, whatever tomorrow might bring. Right now Jesus cares for you – just as he cared for people in the Gospels.

The writer of Hebrews has been stressing the present work of Jesus all the way through this letter. Right now, Jesus is sustaining everything (1:3). Right now, Jesus is owning us as his family without shame (despite the shame we often feel) (2:12–13). Right now, Jesus preaches through the preaching of God's word (2:12; 12:25). Right now, Jesus leads our congregational worship, making it acceptable to God (2:12; 8:1–2; 13:15). Right now, Jesus is helping those who are being tempted (2:18). Right now, Jesus feels compassion for us and mediates grace for our needs (4:14–16). Right now, Jesus is anchoring our faith in heaven (6:19–20). Right now, Jesus is guaranteeing God's commitment to his people (7:22). Right now and forever, Jesus is interceding for us (7:25).

Through the Holy Spirit, Jesus is with us and for us *now* – right here, right now. Jesus is present now speaking through my words to reassure you. Jesus is present in the care you receive from your brothers and sisters. Jesus is present when we take communion, communicating his love in bread and wine. Jesus is present in your life as your helper, your advocate, your counsellor, your comfort. Right now he is sympathising with us in our weakness and providing help when we're in need.

This wonderful shared life of love that Hebrews 13 exhorts us to keep on living is not something we create through our efforts or our rules. It's something Christ creates among us through his death for us and his life among us.

Reflection

Perhaps stepping deeper into church life feels risky. Maybe you fear you'll get hurt. Maybe you will. After all, the church is a family of sinners – like you. But hear Jesus speak: 'Never will I leave you; never will I forsake you' (v. 5). Then perhaps you can respond: 'The Lord is my helper; I will not be afraid' (v. 6).

The first readers of this letter were mostly converts from Judaism. Their Jewish neighbours were urging them to return to Judaism. 'We have an altar, a priest and a sanctuary,' they say. 'What do you have? Nothing. How can you be cleansed from your sins?' The 'strange teachings' of verse 9 may be people in the church who said they could have it both ways – a kind of combo-religion of Judaism and Christianity.

But the verdict of Hebrews is clear: we're never going to have confidence before God through 'ceremonial foods' because they are of 'no benefit' (v. 9).

Instead we're 'strengthened by grace' (v. 9). What does that mean?

The writer of Hebrews has already talked about grace a couple of times. Here's the first: 'Jesus ... suffered death, so that by the grace of God he might taste death for everyone' (2:9). What's grace? Grace is Good Friday. Grace is Jesus suffering death in our place, bearing our sin, cleansing our shame.

Here's the second reference to grace: 'Let us then approach God's throne of grace with confidence, so that we may receive mercy and find grace to help us in our time of need' (4:16). What's grace? Grace is the result of Good Friday. Grace is the welcome we receive when we come to God through Jesus. Don't swap that for an empty ceremony.

Throughout this letter, the writer has been saying we *do* have a priest, a sanctuary and a homeland – in heaven. Even our sacrifice, though offered at Calvary on Good Friday, is now being presented before God in heaven.

We're not missing out! Quite the opposite. Those who despise us are the ones who are missing out (v. 10).

Reflection

On earth you may feel like an *outsider* (v. 13). But in heaven you are an *insider* who can approach God's throne with confidence.

God at the margins   Hebrews 13:11–19

When the people of Israel camped in the wilderness, anyone with a contagious disease had to live outside the camp in what today we would call 'self-isolation'. If they were healed then they had seven more days of self-isolation. When they finally got home they had to wash themselves thoroughly. You were placed in lockdown.

It's a powerful picture of the hostility we face. Holy Saturday is the moment between the disgrace of Good Friday and the victory of Easter Sunday. It's the moment in which we live: marginalised for Christ's sake while we wait for glory. You may feel isolated because of your faith. People may treat you as if you're contaminated. It's tough. Who wants to be seen as a bigot? I don't. But when we fix our eyes on Jesus we see the ultimate outsider who has become the ultimate insider. Jesus died outside the city, but God has raised him to a place of honour.

In the Israelite camp, God was at the centre in the Most Holy Place. Meanwhile, at the margins were sacrificial carcasses and unclean people (v. 11). But at the cross and resurrection, an amazing thing happen: Jesus flipped the whole picture. Now God is on the margins – with sinners, with the unclean, with you. The Holy Place where God dwells is no longer in the temple, but among marginalised sinners. For Jesus is making the contaminated 'holy through his own blood' (v. 12).

The world 'civilisation' comes from the word 'city'. Verse 14 says we live outside the city. We're seen as uncivilised. But we belong to *another* city and our city will last forever (v. 14). It's no hardship to leave behind the earthly city of a dying humanity when you're coming to the heavenly city of the living God!

Meanwhile, every Christian has become a priest through Jesus our high priest. What's our priestly activity? To offer sacrifices. Not sacrifices of atonement – Jesus has done that once for all (as Hebrews has kept reminding us). Our sacrifices are the sacrifice of our lips as we praise God and the sacrifice of our lives as we love others (v. 15–16). Love God and love your neighbour – that's the priestly activity that brings pleasure to God.

Reflection

The sacrifices we offer are lips that praise God and lives that love others. What sacrifices are you going to offer today?

Jesus lives to care for his people   Hebrews 13:20-25

Jesus is not dead! Yes, he died for our sin – really and truly, dead and buried. But on Easter Sunday God *'brought back from the dead our Lord Jesus, that great Shepherd of the sheep'* (v. 20). Jesus lives to care for his people. He's shepherding you right now. Isaiah 40:11 says that when the Lord comes to his people:

> *He tends his flock like a shepherd:*
> *he gathers the lambs in his arms*
> *and carries them close to his heart;*
> *he gently leads those that have young.*

Today Jesus is alive and he gathers you in his arms, carries you close to his heart and gently leads you.

Verse 20 says God brought Jesus back from the dead 'through the blood of the eternal covenant'. The resurrection demonstrates that the sacrifice of Jesus has been accepted. Once a prisoner has served their sentence they can walk free because the law has no more claim on them. Having paid the penalty of our sin in full, death had no further claim on Jesus. The one with an 'indestructible life' could walk free (7:16). And we walk free with him. The new covenant with its promise of forgiveness has been ratified.

And right now Jesus provides for you. These verses are a prayer that God will equip us and work in us 'through Jesus Christ' (v. 21). Jesus has purchased God's blessing and now he gives that blessing to us through the Holy Spirit. Today Jesus is equipping you for the challenges of this week. How will you cope when hardship comes your way? How will you resist temptation when it whispers in your ear? How will you fulfil the tasks God has given you? By asking him to equip you and work in you 'through Jesus Christ'.

Reflection

In verse 22, the writer describes his letter as 'my word of exhortation'. Hebrews is full of amazing truth. But in the end, it's not a treatise or a lecture. It's an exhortation to *'hold firmly to the faith we profess'* (4:14; see also 2:1; 3:6, 14; 4:11; 6:1, 11–12; 10:23–24, 36; 12:1, 15–16), to *'approach God's throne of grace with confidence'* (4:16; see also 10:19–22) and to be fixated on Jesus (3:1; 12:2).

10 Publishing

a division of 10 of those.com

10Publishing is the publishing house of **10ofThose**.
It is committed to producing quality Christian resources
that are biblical and accessible.

www.10ofthose.com is our online retail arm selling
thousands of quality books at discounted prices.

For information contact: **info@10ofthose.com**
or check out our website: **www.10ofthose.com**